30-SECOND MOMENTS

And the Women Who Raised Me

DENISE BARD

ISBN: 979-8-8765-5701-8
Edited by Ernest Bowker
Copyedit and production by Kathryn F. Galán,
    Wynnpix Productions

This book is dedicated to the late educator, Bob Sedia, for always knowing the right words to say to support me and for giving me the raw and honest advice that I needed to hear.
And to the late Susan Satinsky, one of my middle school counselors, who also had such a positive impact on my life and on that of so many others, although I was the only one to tell her what a difference she had made. She inspired my mission to find the women recognized in this book and to remind them of the impact and lasting impressions they have made.

And to the many teachers out there who are also "raising" children whom they don't know they have, thank you!

Contents

Foreword

I have been a high school teacher for over thirty years, and one thing I know to be true about teachers is that we long to make a positive difference in the lives of our students. I am also convinced that the desire to make a difference in the lives of others is a universal one.

At the beginning of my teaching career, I volunteered to teach eighth-grade religion on Sundays in my parish. Denise Bard was in my eighth-grade class. She was always friendly and engaged, but on one particular day, her head was down on the desk. I can still see her mop of beautiful brown curls resting on her arms.

I touched her on the shoulder and asked if she was okay. When she lifted her head, I saw a black eye and the saddest expression in her eyes.

Later, I told the sister in charge of the program what I had observed, and she explained that Denise was temporarily living in Anchor House, a shelter for young people with no safe place to go. I wasn't sure what to do, but I wanted Denise to know that I supported her, so I paid her a brief visit there that weekend.

About fifteen years later, I got an email from Denise. She had gotten married, returned to the area, and wondered if we could get together for lunch.

I agreed, and when we met, she looked very much the same! She said she wanted to thank me for the visit that I'd paid her in Anchor House all of those years ago and to tell me that she still had the small teddy bear I had brought her.

I was so touched! Teachers are constantly planting seeds in the hope something will bloom. It was so affirming for me to know that my small act of kindness had such a lasting effect on her.

Since then, Denise and I have become good friends, and I am inspired at the strength and resilience she has demonstrated, despite the abuse and neglect she experienced consistently throughout her formative years. I cannot imagine what she went through, because the people who were supposed to love, help, and protect her had manipulated and abused her.

She credits that strength and resilience to people like me, who came into her life and made a positive connection. Denise believes these encounters can be as brief as "30-second moments," which reassure the suffering person that he or she is worthy of love and compassion.

By reflecting on and remembering these moments across her young life, Denise was able to shift the focus of her situation, from one of despair and anger to one of hope and peace.

I encouraged Denise to become a motivational speaker, because I believe her story can help and inspire others, as it has helped and inspired me. Despite her traumatic upbringing, she has become a wise and loving wife and mother. I am truly amazed at how wonderful she is with both of her children, one of whom has autism and a host of health issues.

Additionally, Denise now serves on the board of Anchor House, the shelter where she was housed briefly, all of those years ago.

In true Denise style, she has gone beyond my expectations: guest speaking at podcasts, hosting teachers' workshops, and now, writing this book! Her story will inspire you to overcome whatever challenges you face and motivate you to reach out and help someone else.

In this book, Denise gives concrete examples of how people in her life provided relief from the unbearable suffering she experienced every day of her formative years. These people included teachers, babysitters, volunteers, and, in some cases, strangers.

Many were not experts in the field of psychology, education, or social work. Rather, they simply took the time to notice that she was suffering and reached out in whatever way they could, to let her know they cared.

One example that Denise cites came from her third-grade teacher, Miss Kiess. Miss Kiess had asked the class to draw a picture of an activity each student enjoyed doing with their mothers. Denise was humiliated to realize that there was no example of this in her life; her mother only provided moments of abuse and neglect.

As Miss Kiess walked around the room to offer positive feedback on each child's picture, Denise's embarrassment and trepidation grew. She finally drew a picture of herself and her mother in a car, because car rides were generally times of relief from the abuse.

When Miss Kiess bent down to look at Denise's picture, she did not comment. Rather, she looked deeply into Denise's eyes and smiled. This example of a "30-second moment" showed Denise that "…sometimes kindness doesn't need to be spoken in words. Sometimes, it is found in a simple smile."

While teachers have many opportunities to provide these encounters to their students, anyone can provide these "moments" to others. We can all make a real difference in each other's lives. It only takes a compassionate look at another and a decision to reach out to them. While we may not always see the results, these encounters can be truly life-changing for all of us.

This book is a testament to the strength and resilience we can build in one another, if we can just notice and reflect on those moments of sharing that others are willing to give us and then to notice and give those moments to others, in return.

Catherine Sewnig
Retired teacher

Introduction

When I turned twelve, my mother regained full custody of me. I had been living full-time with her for two years. Two years of constant fear of the unknown. Always walking on eggshells, because I never knew what her mood would be or what I would do to set her off.

Two years with a packed bag under my bed, hoping and praying someone would rescue me. Two years of dreaming about a life I would never get. Two years of just being *something*.

I was the something that had ruined her life. I was the something that reminded her she was raped. I was the something that caused everything to go wrong in everyone's life, including the things that happened to me.

I had been something used as a bargaining chip to support someone's drug addiction. I had been something used as a hostage to control someone else's life. I was something to take rage out on. And I was something that was hated.

I was just something. And at the age of fourteen, I no longer wanted to be anything.

How does a kid come to that decision?

How does a kid come to believe they are the problem, that they are the reason for everything that goes wrong?

That they are just something?

How did I go from the something I was to the someone I am?

The woman who has been happily married for twenty-three years. The woman who is a mom to two incredible human beings. The woman who is an advocate for those who don't have a voice and for those who haven't found their voice yet. The woman who sits on the board for the same nonprofit shelter she once called home. The woman who is a keynote speaker and the woman who is now an author.

Well, I'd love to tell you, but first you need to know where my story began…

Chapter One

The Podcast

I recently did a podcast, which I have to say was such an amazing experience.

The host, Ann Kagarise, had questions she'd sent me before the actual interview. In our messaging back and forth, we realized quickly that we shared so many similarities. The crazy ones were how we *felt* in certain moments.

You will always hear me say, "We may not share the same experience, but we can have relatable feelings. We can relate on some level."

Ann's first question, which is what I think most people would also ask, was, "Tell me where your story begins."

Well, it started at birth. But if we really get into it, it started before birth.

I am the product of two drug-addicted teens who came from very dysfunctional families. When I say that, I always get someone who says, "Every family has some dysfunction." Well, I hope it's not as bad as mine.

I have heard stories over the years from outside sources. Some of them are told the same way by multiple people, so I tend to believe those more. I also realize stories can be told from a person's point of view. All of the stories paint a very messy picture.

The stories that were painted of me at an early age were not pretty. Prior to my birth, my mother told me, she didn't know she was pregnant until she was seven months along. I remember being seven months pregnant, myself, so I find that hard to believe.

She would also tell me the story of *how* she was raped. Let me stop here for a second and stress that I will never deny or agree with this story for two reasons. One, I was not there for me to deny it; and two, my mother's depictions and stories are not always consistent.

Again, it's really hard to know what is true and what is not. Especially when, at one point during my early childhood, she was "getting back together" with him (my biological father). All I can say is that, on and off my whole life, when I was still talking to her, she would tell me how I was a "rapist" child. My earliest memory of her saying those words to me was when I was four.

Yes, four years old.

Most of my memories started at that age. There are a couple that I recall from being around three, but they are very quick snippets.

Ann asked me, later in the interview, if my mother used drugs while she was pregnant. *Yes!* Now, what type of drugs, I have no idea. Friends have shared that my mother drank, popped "pills" (not sure what they were), and smoked pot all while she was pregnant. Remember, until the seventh month, she didn't "know."

The "I didn't know part" is another tricky one, because there were people who said she knew, which I honestly believe. The real question that I do not have a solid answer for is whether or not she was on cocaine at that point. That would become her drug of choice.

Now that I've told you all of that, you are probably wondering if I had any problems because of exposure. When I worked with my kids' genetics doctor, her belief is that, based on physical birth defects and medical and learning problems, I was most definitely exposed. And that would make sense, explaining why I have some medical issues that my kids have inherited.

So, getting back to my "where your story begins…" I start to tell my story, the one I know based on my firsthand knowledge, with some added validation from others who knew the situation at the time.

As I've mentioned, I am the product of two addicted teens. I grew up on my mother's side. My father and his family denied my existence at that time. At least that is what I was told.

I can confirm that his mother did, for sure. She even told me so, when we met in 1994 for the first time. She has now spent years apologizing. I did see his father and new wife on several random occasions, and I saw even my father once, which I will get into further.

My mother was sixteen years old when she had me. She dropped out of high school but later got her GED. My earliest memories of my childhood were before I was in preschool. So, the time before that has been described to me by different people who were in and out of the picture. Oh, and through some actual pictures, as well.

In the beginning we lived with my grandmother and four uncles, whose ages ranged from eleven to seventeen. It was a bit chaotic, living in a house full of mostly teens. Although I was very young, I do remember times when my mother was not there.

There were five children in total, four of them boys. My youngest uncle and I are only eleven years apart, so I did spend a lot more time in the same house with him.

One of the stories told to me by my oldest uncle was that he put beer in my baby bottle to get me to stop crying, because he was having a party. If you are shaking your head, I am, too.

Another story I learned as an adult is that any time my mother had me in her care, I would be half dressed, dirty, and with a full diaper. This person expressed her concerns to my mother and grandmother, but nothing changed. Neglect was a big issue, and it's the reason I have a flat spot on the back of my head and an indentation that cannot be explained.

The other random memories I have are of playing with a couple of neighbors on my street. I had my first snotty kiss on a dare with one of them. Another memory was playing Barbies with an older girl down the street.

Here is where my vivid memories start as a very young child. At that time, I was living in my grandmother's house. My mom would visit briefly. When she was home, there was always drama and chaos.

I remember hearing screaming coming from the upstairs bedroom. I sneaked up the steps, and as I peeked through the railing, I saw my grandmother beating my mother. The cycle of abuse.

The house was always filled with some type of screaming and fighting. Total chaos. It was a normal thing. It was what I knew.

I entered preschool at the age of four. There are a few things I think about, when I revisit old memories. The first is one of the days it snowed.

I had worn a dress with little dress shoes. When it was time to go outside, we were supposed to get our boots on. In order to go near the snow, we had to wear boots.

Well, mine had disappeared. Someone had taken them. So, there I was, standing next to a pile of snow on the blacktop.

The teacher said, "Don't you go in that snow."

But my little four-year-old self thought, "Well, if I touch it with my toe, does it really mean I am in it?"

Then, there was summer. We had a relay race, and I fell, scraping my knee pretty bad.

Okay, so, I say it was bad, but if it was like the scrapes my kids used to get, I might be a little over-dramatic.

The teacher picked me up and took me to the bathroom to clean me up. This was in the seventies, so the lights used to hang from a wire above, and there was always a yellow hue.

I stood on the table while she cleaned my scrape and put on a Band-Aid. That was the first time I remember feeling what I had always longed for. The first time I remember what it felt like to have someone "care for me." I mean true caring, something I had not known before.

The rest of my memories during that time are not the best. In fact, it was the start of the worst.

Chapter Two

It Begins

My mother used to come to pick me up from preschool with random men. One day, I remember getting in the car with some guy I had never seen before. I sat on my mother's lap. This was back when we didn't need to use seat belts, and you could literally sit wherever you wanted.

The window was down, and I had my hand out. I remember wanting to get out of that car. The feeling was unsettling. The pounding of my heart was deafening.

My mother was smoking a cigarette, and when she went to flick off the ashes in the ashtray, some settled on the top of one of my hands. My mother giggled as I jerked my arm back.

My other hand continued to reach out the window, wanting to get out. As she rolled up the glass, she caught my fingers. In those days, we had to crank a car window to roll it up or down. There was no way she didn't see my hand hanging outside the car.

When I cried out, I still remember her laugh as she commented, "You shouldn't have had your hand there."

I knew, when they picked me up, I would not be going "home" to my grandmother's house. It didn't work like that.

I can still remember pulling up to the man's house, a little, white, one-story stucco house. Inside were arched doorways. In the doorway into the kitchen, he had a bar he used with ankle holders, so he could hang upside down and do crunches. How do I know this? He said I should try it.

I can tell you where each room was in relation to the living room—especially the bedroom. This house was one of the worst memories I have. There are many more, but this one suffocates me. There are certain times in life when we can remember everything about a place or time. Where smells, sounds, and touch can bring you into the moment as if it were right now. It's the place where all of my triggers stem from.

Night one, I pulled the covers up, trying to hide. But that is hard to do when I was in the same bed as them. The sheets were moving, and I couldn't hide in the dark. The sounds played over and over in my head. The smell tells the story. I wanted to cry, but I knew I couldn't. Time stands still when you are in fear as a four-year-old.

Night two, I managed to sleep on the couch. I tried covering my head and ears, so I wouldn't hear the sounds, but they still could be faintly heard.

When the sun came up, I heard him call my name. Frozen, I sat there. Heart pounding out of my chest. I didn't want to go in there.

But the anger that came through the firmness in his voice made me leap up. Slowly, I walked. Heart still pounding.

He pointed to the bottom right side of the bed for me to stand. "Watch me 'tickle' your mom."

I closed my eyes, but again, the firm voice ordered, "Watch."

I begged her to let me go "home," to my grandmother's. I don't remember the rest.

No matter how many times I share that memory, it still feels like I am in the moment.

Have you ever had one of those experiences where you can smell the aroma as if it's all around you? Where every detail, all of a sudden, becomes so crisp, it's like you are looking at it? Awful, right!?

Chapter Three

Kinship Care: A Game Of Chess

When I was five years old, family court put me in Kinship Care with my grandmother. For those who do not know what Kinship Care is, well, in short, it is family foster care. Instead of being placed in the foster care system, family court starts with the family. Family court tossed me back and forth between my mother and grandmother for six years.

The story I was told by my grandmother was that, one day, my biological grandfather (her ex-husband) called and said, if she wanted to see me alive, she'd better get over to the apartment where we lived. She was told that my mother had chased him with an ax, although a knife sounds more reasonable.

I remember this apartment well. It was on the second floor. That part of the block had a strip of stores on the ground floor with apartments over top. This was a one-bedroom apartment. As soon as you entered, you were in the kitchen. You walked down the hallway and entered the living room. The fire escape was right outside the living room windows. I played out there often. My mom would also take me out there during what I would assume were her highs.

The apartment was the place where, when I was age four, she stood me on a chair at the stove to "cook" the steak. This was also the place, as told by another uncle, where I would roll joints for them, because I had tiny hands and made them the best. This was also the place where I would see kilos of cocaine and scales lined up, part of a running business. And this was the place where she would leave me alone.

Neglect happened often. I must have stayed alone more times than I can count, at the young age of four. I remember one particular day when she had to run an "errand." I later learned her "errands" were drug-related. Someone was supposed to watch me, she explained, but they never showed.

She taught me how to lock the door behind her. I had to climb on a chair to reach the lock. She said she would be back. Not long after she left, there would be a knock at the door. It was the guy from upstairs. I am not sure why I opened the door, but I did. My next memory has him sitting on the floor next to me, watching *Sesame Street*.

My mother came home to an unlocked door. When she got to the living room, she saw him and grabbed the Coke bottle filled with blue water that I had made the day prior, at the Italian Lights Festival, and she threw it at me. It missed but broke when it hit the floor. I hated that rug. The permanent blue stain reminded me of that day.

Another story told by her friend (or then friend; I will call her PS for privacy) was about one day when PS went over and saw my mother hanging over the fire escape in a raging high. PS kept calling up to her (we were on the second floor), saying, "Just give me the baby."

I remember always feeling safe with PS. She said she was afraid my mother would shut me in the toy box. Which, honestly, was not shocking. She'd hidden me in closets and toy boxes before.

Safe to say, the call to put me in Kinship Care was a good one. At least for that abusive situation. My grandmother had her own struggles, though. She was known to not be a faithful person, if you get what I mean.

She was also a very manipulative woman. I was used as a hostage to control someone else's life. I became the pawn in a game of chess between the two of them that I did not want to play.

Chapter Four

Willingboro

At the age of five, I started kindergarten in Willingboro, New Jersey, after moving in with my grandparents. My mother went in and out of drug rehabs and psychiatric facilities during this time.

When she was in my life, things stayed the same. Random men and random places. It wasn't just white-stucco houses that triggered me. Trailers, junk yards, garages, and the smell of wet dogs fell onto the ever-growing list of triggers.

This was about the time when I was drilled to keep secrets. It would be, "If you tell, you will be taken away and given to someone who will hurt you." She made this our normal, and I was viewed as a "cry baby." The infamous blame game, when the adults in the room tell you everything happening to you is your fault.

The three words that can silence any child are *It's your fault*. Those three words bring on shame and guilt that you've done something wrong.

During the podcast interview, I mentioned to Ann a particular caseworker I had. I will talk more about her later, but I want to mention one very important fact about her right now. She is the first person who told me, "It is not your fault."

Ann referenced the movie *Good Will Hunting*, where Robin Williams's character repeats those words over and over to Matt Damon, causing Matt's character to become overly emotional. It seems fair to say that any of us who have faced some sort of trauma would break, hearing someone continually say those words, "It's not your fault. It's not your fault. It's not your fault."

This is the house where I looked the devil in the eyes. An image that is so searing to this day, one I relive every time I tell it.

My mother was going through withdrawal. That particular night, she slept over, and we shared the bed in my room. I had a twin bed, but, because I was small, there should have been enough room for both of us. Oh, but there wasn't.

During the night, my mother literally kicked me off the bed onto the floor. I remember standing up and reaching to get back in, but she told me she was cold, and I wasn't allowed back in that bed. So, there I lay, on the floor all night. No covers or pillow to lie on.

The next morning, her withdrawal got worse. As I followed her down the hall toward the kitchen, she suddenly stopped, causing me to run right into her back. She quickly whipped around and there I stood, staring directly into the devil's eyes. It was a look I hadn't seen, and I'd seen plenty of things before. It was like her eyes cut right through me.

She was really skinny, so when her hand went up, I knew the feeling of bones were about to come down on me. It was like having a skeleton hit you. I used to have nightmares about that moment.

That was also my fault. Truthfully, it probably was, because I actually remember what caused her to reenter rehab.

My grandmother's house was across the street from a grocery store. We would go out the back door, through a wall of trees, and cross a street to get there. One day, while walking across, my grandmother was asking me something.

I vividly remember telling her that my mother was, "Sniffing the medicine powder through a money straw."

My mother used to tell me it was her medicine. I guess that is one way of looking at it.

My mother took it out on me, because I'd told on her. It was literally like being around a grown child who had massive "tantrums."

Chapter Five

Lalor Elementary School

I was going into the first grade when we moved from Willingboro to Trenton.

It was the first week of school. When I got there, my new first-grade teacher brought me to the bookshelf, pointed to the books, and asked me what book I was reading or wanted to read. I must have panicked, because the heart pounding started again.

I looked around and noticed the kids looking to see which book I would choose.

I'll never forget Ms. Gaudette looking at me and asking, "You don't know how to read, do you?"

My prior elementary school didn't teach reading until the first grade. But at Lalor Elementary in Trenton, reading was taught in kindergarten.

Needless to say, I then had to repeat kindergarten. I remember crying on that first day. I sat at the round table with my head buried in my arm, sobbing. The teacher tried to comfort me, but I was trapped in that moment.

However, I do remember her glancing over during the lesson that she continued to teach the class. Eventually, I warmed up.

I loved elementary school, and I was a good kid. I made honor roll all but one time in fifth grade. I was never good with math. Outside of talking too much, though, I never got into trouble. Those were some of my good childhood memories. The ones during the school day.

Lalor Elementary was a very old school. I mean it even smelled old. This will sound crazy, but that smell to me was the smell of safety. Back in the eighties, there was only one class per grade, which I think helped it to feel more intimate, for a lack of better words. Teachers knew every student, even those not in their class.

I am sure anyone looking back during those years can list off all the favorite things they loved, like recess. There was kickball (I was one of the girls who always was chosen first—I was such a tomboy) and swinging on the swing set as high as you can go and then jumping off onto the blacktop, hoping would make a good landing. There were seesaw catapults, which sucked to play on, if you were the small kid. I also remember how two lunch aides would yell at us for being too "disorderly."

When I look back on the few pictures I have from that time, I can smile, because I see the "happy" me at school. Even though there was chaos at home, at school I was able to be just a kid.

I know the school was aware of the situation in my family. There were several times when I was able to "cool off" in the office during recess with the only air conditioner. I can still see the secretary, Mrs. Keegan's, smile. I would sit in the chair near her desk, and we would just talk. She would ask me how the day was or what I was doing in class. Maybe she asked me things that had to do with home, but I don't remember.

The first time I remember people coming into the school to ask me questions about things at home, I was in either third or fourth grade. I don't remember if it was a school counselor or office person who came with me to an empty classroom on the second floor.

My memories of the questions are vague, however I do remember knowing that I had to be careful with my answers, or I would get taken away or be in trouble. That's what I had been told at home.

Chapter Six

Miss. Kiess

When I was in third grade, my mother must have proven to the court or to my grandmother that she was capable, again, of raising me. So, I moved from my grandmother's house in Trenton to a home in Ewing.

This house was owned by an older woman, Ms. Rue, who rented out two bedrooms of her small, brick house. One bedroom was rented to an older gentleman, and the other was ours. The basement shower and bathroom were what we used. There was a TV and couch down there, as well.

Since I'd moved from Trenton, of course I had to change schools again. This was the third school I had attended. I would only be there for about a month or so. Not sure what happened, but I ended up back at my grandmother's and the school that I loved, where all my friends were.

My teacher that year was Miss Kiess. She had blonde hair and used to wear "fancy" clothes. By fancy, I mean not the jean skirts every teacher was wearing at that time. She would wear white pants and floral tops. I remember one of her dresses had flowers and the fabric crisscrossed in the front, like a robe. It's crazy to me, the details I remember.

I loved Miss Kiess, yet she scared me at the same time. But it was not like the scared I felt at home. It was more of the, "Stop talking or you will be in trouble," kind of fear. I had a knack for being a chatterbox. Really, ask anyone, and they will tell you stories.

There is one day of that school year that stands out to me most. It was around Mother's Day, and Miss Kiess asked the class to draw a picture of what we most loved to do with our moms. The weight I felt in my chest pressed all the air out of my lungs. There was nothing I liked to do with my mom. Plus, my mom was, again, either in rehab or in a drugged-out state.

I looked around the room. All of my friends were busy drawing pictures and coloring in bright colors. I was frantically thinking, *What can I draw?* The only thing I knew—a pitiful rendition of a car with two stick figures. Art wasn't my strongest area.

I watched as Miss Kiess walked around the room, stopping at each desk. She would look at their pictures and then ask them why they loved doing that together.

My heart was pounding as I saw her get closer to my desk. You know when you get that lump in your throat? Mine was as hard as a rock.

She finally got to my desk, looked at the picture, and kneeled down. Well, what was I going to say? I needed to come up with something other than, "It's the only time I feel safe."

But she didn't ask me. She looked at the picture one more time, turned, and looked into my eyes. You know that somewhat awkward feeling you get when someone looks you dead in the eyes?

She didn't ask. It was like she saw *me* and then smiled. It was that feeling of, *no words were needed*. She stood up and walked to the next desk. I took a deep breath and let it out.

For the rest of the day, I didn't feel the ache I usually did when it came to that time of year. For the rest of the day, any time Miss Kiess would look my way, I felt that moment, that eye contact, and immediately smiled.

After that, she was my absolute favorite. Even if she did sometimes scare me by being stern. I believe she got engaged that year and became Mrs. McConnell. I want to say he proposed in our class, but I could totally be wrong.

During the first week after school ended, I remember writing her a letter. I told her she was my favorite teacher. I wrote all the things that were fun that year. I also wrote how she was pretty and nice (I might even have included how I liked her clothes.).

The last thing I wrote before putting my name was, "I wish I had a mom like you." Or I might have written it, "I wish you were my mom." Either way I said it, it was clearly written, how I felt.

My neighbor's dad, who was a stay-at-home dad, helped me to look up her name in the phone book. Yeah, that really ages me right there. I found a Karen Kiess, wrote the address on an envelope, and mailed it. John, my neighbor, never saw what I wrote. He just helped me mail it off.

I am not sure if it ever got to her or if it was to a different Karen Kiess. She never acknowledged it after we went back to school. And back then, there was only one class per grade, and our fourth-grade classroom was right next door to hers. So, there was plenty of opportunity for her to acknowledge that she received it. If ever I had the chance to tell her, I would say…

Thank you for teaching me to know that, sometimes, kindness doesn't need to be spoken in words. Sometimes, it is found in a simple smile. Not all things need to be loud.

Chapter Seven

Florida

The summer before fourth grade, my mother went down to live in Florida, in what she called "a trailer park." I remember her calling once, and she seemed out of breath. She said she was exercising, but I knew she was lying. I remember what that sound indicated.

At one point in the summer, she came up to visit. I remember her telling me, while she was staying there, "If anyone calls, I am not your mom." I was coached to say that I was her sister. It didn't make sense to me, but then again, nothing ever made sense with her.

I think this was also the time she drilled me on what to say to the social worker she had an appointment with. My mother drove a blue car with a white convertible top. I remember she kept driving around a circle (roundabout), going over and over what my responses were to any questions I would get. If I did not listen, she told me I would never see her again. So, round and round we went, until I could repeat it, word for word.

I don't remember any social workers ever asking me about good touch and bad touch. I don't think we learned about that back then. I don't think it would have mattered. When I was around ten, my mother and grandmother handed me this book, *Where Do Babies Come From?* It was a very colorful cartoon book explaining the birds and the bees. The pictures depicted "things" that I saw. It just reinforced what I was always told "is all normal."

That visit to the social worker allowed my mother unsupervised visits. This was when she took me back to Florida with her for a week. This is also when I learned the lie, to say that she was living in a trailer. Really, she was living in a small camper with a guy, plus an *old* man and his dog.

Times didn't change when it came to where I slept. The sights, sounds, and smell were constant reminders of why I never really wanted to go with her anywhere.

There are a few things I remember from that visit. The sleeping arrangements. One night, with them. The next, with the old man and his dog, and so forth. I also remember meeting kids and playing with them, as much as I could.

One day around dinner time, their dad called for them. The dad said to me they would be back after they ate dinner. He was in the doorway of their camper. I could see in it. It was bigger and much nicer than where I was staying.

As he shut the door, I sat down to wait. He saw me and then said I should go home and eat, too. The problem was there wasn't anything to eat. Of course, I didn't say that. I told him I would just wait there, instead.

He paused for a second and then asked if I wanted to come in to eat with them. *Yes*! I jumped up.

During some outings with my mom, we walked everywhere. I don't remember there ever being a car. On one of those walks, we passed by an elementary school. She told me that was where I would be going to school.

This scared me, because I didn't want to stay with her. Plus, this was only a visit. But somehow, she believed she would be getting custody of me again. Thankfully, that didn't happen.

On one of my last nights in Florida, I remember our going to a party at the small home of the park's office manager. Her name was Renee. Again, crazy how I can remember things.

What I remember about that night was how she kept looking over at me. Even though the room was filled with people smoking pot and doing whatever, I believe she knew I should not be there, exposed to this.

I returned to New Jersey thereafter.

Chapter Eight

Val

Over the course of those six years, I lived with my grandmother and stayed in Lalor Elementary School, except for that temporary move in third grade. During those six years, I had a babysitter who lived just around the corner. I'm not sure how my grandmother connected with her to take care of me, but somehow it worked.

Val's house was definitely a safe house. All the kids in the neighborhood (even the ones with good homes) always found their way to her house. Her daughter was about a year old (seven years between us).

She had a swing set and a kiddie pool in the yard. Inside, she had a large, built-in bookcase filled with books like *The Berenstain Bears*. I didn't have books at home and didn't really like to read. It was difficult to stay focused, which I would learn as an adult was because I have dyslexia and ADHD. For some reason, though, I loved these books. I know there were others, but I tended to go straight for those.

I am sure, if any of us got together today, we would all talk about our favorite game we loved to play: hide-and-seek in the house. We were still playing that game into double digits. Val would always be it, and when she found one of us, everyone would know, because she would tickle us to death, bringing on the loudest laughter.

Then there was the scrambled eggs and cheese. No one makes scrambled eggs and cheese like Val. I can't ever get them to taste the same.

Oh, and then there were the bike rides. *All* the kids would go on these with her. Actually, most of the time, we would knock on her door and ask if she could take us on a bike ride. It was like asking her to come out and play. She would always oblige. She had a little seat on the back of her bike for her daughter to sit in.

The best rides were going to McDonald's. Happy Meal, cheeseburger, fries, Coke, and a sundae.

One of the last rides I remember was to McDonald's. This particular time, there was no one else except Val, her daughter, and me. That day, my grandmother and mom were going to court over my custody battle.

I remember, clear as day, sitting outside of McDonald's at a round stone table. While we were eating, Val asked me, "How would you feel about your mom getting you back?"

I can't remember what I said, but it wasn't how happy or excited I was for that to happen. I do remember a sour pit in my stomach and a lump in the middle of my chest.

It was already hard to be around my mother and pretend everything was normal to keep the peace. Now, I would have to do it every day. That was a lot of pretending to do.

I will always remember that day, because it was the first time someone whom I trusted asked me how I felt. Not that I said what was happening. I'd seen what happens to people when you start to open up to them.

As an adult, Val shared with me that she knew something was not right and how, anytime someone tried to help, they were pushed away. She said the only thing she could do was to give me a safe place to go.

And it was safe. Val gave me great childhood memories to look back on. If it weren't for her, I would not have any during those years.

Val,

Thank you for teaching me that sometimes the rescue comes in the form of compassion and kindness. For teaching me what it looks like when you make your child a priority. Even as an adult, I continue to learn.

I watch the connections and memories you make with your daughter. It gives me the examples I need to know, for how to give the same to my daughter.

Chapter Nine

Mrs. Kessler

Mrs. Kessler was my middle-school counselor for sixth and seventh grade. I remember the first time I met her. I got those butterflies in my stomach. I would get them whenever I met someone whom I could immediately picture as being "a mom."

My thoughts were, "She's so nice. She is pretty. She always smiles." Those were three characteristics that checked off my mom box.

I have to assume my elementary school gave her a heads-up about me. I don't think a counselor just picks someone out by looking at them and says, "Yup, that kid needs help."

So, the first meeting with her is a bit fuzzy. Most of my thoughts are of this person who I so badly wished would rescue me.

During sixth grade, I don't remember a lot of our interactions. She would call me down to her office to "check in" on me. I do know, when I saw her in the hall, I immediately smiled, and she always acknowledged me. Which, for a kid like me, made me feel seen.

Sixth grade is a weird year. You go from being in a smaller elementary school, where everyone knows everyone, to being in a larger school. There were days when I wouldn't see anyone I went to elementary school with.

Everyone is just trying to find their place. Where do they fit in? I always struggled with that. Where do I fit in? Even today, I sometimes ask that question.

Sixth grade was also the year I moved in with my mom, full-time. Which meant I was going through new (and old) challenges at home. It was the beginning of what would become a storm. I lost all of the things that were familiar to me. I went back to surviving and treading water in the unknown.

At home, it was always a ticking time bomb. You never knew when it would explode or what you did to cause it. The phrase often used to describe this is, "walking on eggshells." The eggshells I walked on were not hard at all. Cracking daily.

I would hear at least one of these phrases regularly:

"You are the reason I don't have..."

"You should be happy I don't treat you like your grandmother treated me."

"I wish you were (someone else we know)."

"No one wants to hear you."

"You are such a crybaby."

"I hate you."

And the best one was, "I never wanted you."

Imagine hearing one or more of those *every day* and then having to go to school to try to fit in with a population of kids that came from "good" homes. Before you say, "You don't know what they are facing," I don't. But what I do know is those kids whom I desperately wanted to fit in with had parents who didn't want me to fit in with them, because of where I came from.

I spent so many nights sitting on the edge of my bed, looking out the window with my headphones on as loud as they would go, daydreaming of what it would be like if someone would just come and rescue me. A little piece of you dies every day that goes by with no one in sight.

During the podcast with Ann, I was talking to her about this part of my story. She told me of a poem she wrote when she was younger, possibly close to the age I was at that time. Have you ever read or heard something that, if you didn't know better, you could believe you wrote or said it? This was one of those moments—it raised the hair on my arms. The shared emotional experience is undeniable.

Hearing her share this poem was as if she was looking through my eyes. It was the first time I heard someone share the same heartache. Share the same wishful secret.

I never shared with anyone how I would envision a family of my own. I never told a soul that I would take cutouts of soap-opera stars and put them in my wallet, to imagine they were my parents, just so I could find a little hope.

Poem
By Ann Kagarise

I remember many a night
When I would pray in the midst of fright
To a God I did not know or understand;
Who I wished would reach down with a
    gentle hand,
Wipe away my tears of desperation,
Rescue me from my world of isolation,
From the four walls in which I dwelled.
Looking out the window from a world I
    knew well
Wondering exactly what it would be like
To be in one of those other bedrooms still
    lit by light.
I would stare at them through the hazy mist
    from my breath
Till their lights went out as though it were
    a death…

A death of a dream that gave me hope
That in the midst of chaos would help me
    cope.
Laying back down with a tear on my cheek
Praying, Father, I lay me down to sleep
In hopes for a new family in which I seek.
I know I don't know who they are,
But I pray with much faith that they are not
    very far!

During middle school, I was still close with my two best friends from elementary school. We had all ventured out to explore additional friendships like most kids do, going into middle school. There was a group of friends I started hanging out with who were not "bad" kids, but they had some freedoms—or should I say, access to things most at that age don't have. Alcohol.

Because of how I was treated at home, I did everything I could to stay away. That meant finding friends I could stay with, especially on the weekends. Most of the time, I stayed with my elementary school best friends. At times, I practically lived at their houses. When they weren't home, I spent time with the new friends I'd made.

I remember drinking for the first time (outside of the baby bottle full of beer my uncle gave me when I was a year old). It was over the weekend, and we went to my friend's uncle's house.

My first drink really would become my drink of choice: a Screwdriver. That drink would one day almost become the death of me.

I found, like I think a lot of people do, that I was less afraid, less anxious, and had a numbness, when I drank. I could relax, which was something I could never do at home. Remember, I was only twelve years old when I started.

This was also about the time when I sometimes got argumentative with teachers. As a matter of fact, in sixth grade, my social studies teacher gave me an award for being the "lawyer" of the year, or maybe someone who will be a lawyer, someday. She said I could make an argument out of anything.

It was true. But those arguments got me attention from teachers. Was it the right attention? No. But it was something. And that something would have me called down to Mrs. Kessler's room for her to "check in" with me. Most people, or should I say most teachers, think that kids who have those argumentative behaviors are just bad kids. Truth is, a lot of us have abandonment issues. We are either trying to get it over with or we are seeing who really sees more in us then just a "troubled" kid. So, it's basically a test.

This went on for two years. In that time, I also began fighting. Physically fighting. Sometimes alongside a group of friends I'd made. This was just another outlet for me. No excuse; just telling you how I dealt with my feelings.

I never got into trouble at home for fighting. My mother would just ask whether I'd kicked the other person's ass. Only once did I say, "No."

I ended up in a fight with one of my elementary school best friends. She literally kicked my ass. Her mom taught me how to fight when I was younger, because I was little and did need to defend myself. The fight began over something dumb and was really egged on by an older neighborhood kid.

After that fight, a police officer came to my door to talk to me about it. Before he left, he said, "See you later, Tyson," which made me laugh, because I was no match for my friend. She was the Tyson.

The next day at school, my friend and I were called to the Vice Principal's office. I think the school was concerned that we would start fighting in class. To be honest, I am not sure how it happened, but we made up and things went back to normal, with us being the close friends we had been before. Maybe even closer.

During another podcast with Ann, we talked about Fight-or-Flight. Back as a kid, I didn't know what this term meant, but I sure did live it.

Again, fighting was something I craved. I would fight every chance I got. It was like letting out all of the frustration and anger with every punch. It got to the point where, if a person was a problem for someone, they would come to me and ask if I would fight the person, and I *did*! Looking back through the only middle-school yearbook I have, people were writing names for me to "get" for them. It is embarrassing to be remembered that way.

At home, those loud screams from my mother would often turn into her hitting or pushing me. I was just so angry back then. What I found was, if I laughed every time she hit me, she would stop and say, "There is something seriously wrong with you." The harder she hit, the harder I laughed, and the sooner it was over. I learned to survive in that situation.

At almost the end of the year, one day, I was watching TV and playing with a little suction cup toy. (It would be considered a fidget today.) I had it under my eye when it sucked down. I pulled it off, causing a bruise.

After realizing what I had done and seeing the mark, two things went through my head. First of all, *Holy Shit*, and then second, *this might be my chance.*

See, up until that day, I'd never had any bruises that were visible, except in elementary school, but they were always brushed off as bruises from kickball or falling off my bike. I didn't have anything that I thought would lead someone to ask, "What is happening at home?"

No one specifically asked me that question. Not saying I would tell the truth, since again, I was convinced all of it was normal, and it was my own fault it was happening. But what if I said, "It doesn't matter, because I know it was my fault"?

The next day at school, I tried to hide it but didn't. It was a cat-and-mouse game. One minute, I wanted someone to ask what happened, and the next, I wanted to hide so no one would see.

Well, it was my science teacher who saw it and told Mrs. Kessler. I was called to her office. I remember sitting on the couch, with her across from me on her chair. She asked what had happened to my eye. I froze. Heart pounding so hard that not only could I feel it pounding, but I could also hear it pounding.

"My uncle and I were playing, and when he tossed (something), it got me in the face." That's all I could think to say. I didn't want to say I was playing with a toy. Although, looking back, I wish I'd had the courage to say something other than what I said. This, of course, caused a chain reaction.

I can't remember if it was that day or the next, but after I got home to the apartment, someone came to the door. It was a guy who asked if my mother was home.

I told him she was not. He handed me a card. It said DYFS (Division of Youth and Family Services). He said, "Have your mom call me."

At that moment, my heart was pounding so hard. I was so scared. I knew what would happen, and I had to figure out how to survive it.

Heart pounding, mind racing. What should I say? What should I do?

One part was, this is my chance. Be brave and say something. And the other part was, no, you can't. You will just get into trouble, because this is a normal thing that everyone does, and you caused this to yourself (by not talking about the toy and the bruise).

Later that day, he came to the house. By this time, my grandmother had come over, too. Not a good sign. Growing up, anytime there was someone or something that would threaten their control or if it was a chance for me to be rescued, they would come together as a unit to shut it down. This time was no exception. No one would be taking me away from them.

We went to the kitchen table. It was a small one-bedroom apartment, so there was a wall separating the kitchen from the living room. My grandmother and mother sat on the couch, just on the other side of the wall closest to the door.

He asked me questions, and I answered according to how I was "supposed to" answer. There was a small piece of paper he used to write things down.

I pulled it over to me, grabbed his pen, and wrote, "Please help me. I'm scared."

He looked down at it and read it. Looked at me and nodded. The next thing I remember is him walking out the door and never hearing from him or anyone about this ever again. That glimmer of hope to be rescued disappeared as the door closed behind him.

I was so close. I'd finally had the courage to put something down. When I tell you this was crushing, it was like having a rock tied to your ankle and being thrown into the river. Slowly you sink to the bottom, and all the air you have is gone.

The end of the year came, and I wrote Mrs. Kessler a letter. I told her how I was sorry about lying to her about how I'd gotten the bruise. I told her how much I liked her and that I hoped she could forgive me. It was hard to be around her with her possibly seeing me as a liar. All I could think of was, she saw me like my mother did. She saw me as a liar and an attention-seeker.

I have tried many times over the years to find Mrs. Kessler, just to be able to tell her this:

Your impact on my life is immeasurable. You gave me something to look forward to every day, when I came to school. You saw me. You saw the hurt that was always meant to be hidden inside. Most importantly, thank you for trying to rescue me and giving me the courage to find a tiny piece of my voice. Because of that,

I was able to stand up for myself, even if it was in a small way.

Thank you for unknowingly stepping into the role of a "temporary" mom, teaching me that sometimes the rescue isn't in the physical sense. Sometimes, the rescue is in finding the strength to use that voice that has always been inside of me.

Mrs. Kessler

Chapter Ten

Anchor House

In eighth grade, my neighborhood's middle school was switched to a brand-new school. Apparently, we were told, our neighborhood was not wanted at our old school. We lived in Trenton, but our side of the street went to the Hamilton schools. Once again, this new school and new counselor were told ahead of time about me.

I had been living full-time with my mother for two years. Two years of constant fear of the unknown. Always walking on eggshells, because I never knew what her mood would be or what I would do to set her off. Two years with a packed bag under my bed, hoping and praying someone would rescue me. Two years of dreaming about a life I would never get. Two years of just being something.

I had been something that ruined her life. I had been something that reminded her she was raped. I had been the something that caused everything to go wrong in everyone's life, including the things that happened to me. I had been something used as a bargaining chip to support someone's drug addiction. I had been used as a bargaining chip to control someone else's life. I was something to take rage out on. And I was something that was hated.

One month into that school year, I no longer wanted to be anything. I couldn't live this way. I felt so broken and defeated.

One morning, before school, I woke up and said, "I'm done." I went to the medicine cabinet and grabbed the bottles of prescription meds that she was clearly addicted to. I took a couple of each and crushed them into water. Without hesitation, I started to drink.

But after that first sip, I stopped. The thought was clear as day. If I do this, they (my mother and grandmother) were going to claim to be the victims. That was the only reason I stopped.

I was ready to end it all, but that thought changed everything. I walked to the bus stop and told my friend Angela, since I had already taken a gulp of my little "cocktail." I wasn't sure if it would have any effect. I also knew she would tell the school, and maybe I would have the courage to tell more.

Sure enough, she did. I was called down to the guidance counselor's office. The police were called, and, of course, my mother was called. She did exactly what I'd expected her to do.

She played the victim, telling them she did everything for me and that I had a good life, so there must be something mentally wrong with me, and I needed help.

Before any words could come out of the counselor's or the officer's mouth, I said, point blank, "I am not going home with her." It was the first time I'd had any courage to speak up for myself when someone with authority was in the room.

I was not going to go home. I didn't care where they took me, but if they tried to force me to go home with her, I would either follow through with my decision or I would run.

I am not sure how the decision was made, but I would find myself standing at the door to a nonprofit shelter called Anchor House. It is a shelter for runaway, abused, and homeless youth. I clearly fit into the abused category, although I am sure my mother would say differently.

Little did I know that the trajectory of my life was about to change. I would go from being "something" to becoming "someone."

I remember the exact feeling when I walked in. It was so immediate. I felt as if I had been holding my breath underwater and came up for a deep breath of air. My body went from being so tight from fear to one of calm and safety. I was no longer afraid, at that moment. It's a feeling that is hard to describe to someone, if they have never felt fear every second of every day of their life.

Anchor House is a converted convent. The bedrooms have a bathroom that connects two rooms together (Jack and Jill bathroom). There were two beds in each room, and each kid had a dresser.

My bedroom was number 2 and I was in bed number 2. Not sure if there were really numbers to the beds, but I just recall calling it bed two.

The girl I shared a room with was older and left a few days after I got there. I had a total of three roommates while I lived there. At the time I was there, there were a total of twelve kids, ranging in ages from nine to seventeen years old.

I can remember the first night. It was the first time I didn't sleep with a pillow over my head. Since I was little, I would cover my head to drown out the sounds that would be either next to me in bed or in the same room. I was terrified of what I might hear, what I might see, or what I would be forced to see. But there, I had no fears.

I dreaded facing the day with my mom. I did not have to worry about walking on eggshells while I was at the shelter. For the first time, I woke up with the feeling of freedom.

Anchor House gave me the ability to just be a kid. I didn't have to worry about what would set someone off or what I would need to do to get through it. I was seen, heard, and cared about without any agenda. I really got to experience a lot of firsts.

Every night, we would eat at the long dinner table together. This was where the adults (counselors) would start discussions, such as how was everyone's day or little things like that. And we would all have chores to do, which would alternate weekly. Most of the kids groaned at chores, but, honestly, I loved them. There was a feeling of being in a family, having to do them. Unless you got bathrooms, then yes. I would groan, too!

There were also outings, which volunteers took us on. One of those outings was to a Flyers hockey game. In order to be permitted to go, you had to be on good behavior. Most all of us were able to go except for my roommate, Sheena. The night before, she hid a chocolate bar from Ms. Pat, one of the volunteers. Man, did I have the best laughs with her. She always looked out for me, as did all of the other girls. I think about each of them often.

Volunteers were a big part of the shelter. They helped fill in the areas where staff couldn't be available. For instance, when you first get to Anchor House, you are taken to the doctor for a quick check up. Joan was the volunteer who took me and a younger boy.

I will never forget Joan and what she did for me. While I was at Anchor House, my great-grandmother passed away. My mother showed up that day to tell me she was gone, and then she told me it was my fault for causing her stress by lying about everything.

I turned to run. Part in anger, and part in heartache. Joan happened to hear what she said. So, she grabbed my hand and pulled me into a small room, sat me down, and put her arm around me, while telling me everything will be okay.

Within seconds, the feeling of being alone was gone.

I had always had to face things alone and never had that feeling of someone being there for me. Finally, someone was there.

Chapter Eleven

Michelle

The first person I met when I got to Anchor House was Michelle. She would be my case manager and counselor.

We walked into a small room and sat across from each other. When you hear people say things like, "Things happen for a reason," or "It was meant to be," this was one of those times. She would be the person who literally changed my life forever.

After the meet and greet, learning about Anchor House and the expectations and rules, Michelle stood up and threw her arms out wide. Honestly, I think I stood there, frozen, not sure what to do. She would probably tell you the same thing.

Then, she wrapped her arms around me and squeezed me so tight, it felt like all of the fear and sadness disappeared in that moment.

Michelle tells the story of how she could tell I was afraid of hugs. What does that mean? It means that hugs to me were forced up to then, either by someone else with an agenda or by me, because of how I was taught. This hug, though, was not forced, as it may seem from my writing. It was really a scoop to say, "You are safe."

Needless to say, I would find her any chance I could, to get one of her hugs. Even to this day, she is still in my life. I can say there has never been anyone who came close to a Michelle hug.

At Anchor House, we had a lot of counseling sessions. Michelle would call me into one of the counseling rooms, usually every day or when she was working. And I would always get excited. Not because I wanted counseling, but because I would get one of her hugs.

The counseling part was a bit difficult for me. How do I talk about things when I have been trained my whole life that, one, everything that happened to me was normal, and two, I was always told to stop being so dramatic or a crybaby, and three, things were my fault. And the embarrassment and shame that came along with that.

I was still suffocated by secrets that could never be shared. Even with Michelle, whom I trusted and had grown to love, because of her unconditional love for me. I had watched people leave my life over the years and been told it was my fault, because I was too much for them. I did not want Michelle to leave me. So, I held a lot inside.

I can say I don't really remember the discussions at all. But I do remember three things she always said to me. One was that the things that happened to me were not my fault. How did she know what those things were? I never told her. Yet, she would always say it to me. Maybe it was a way to try to make me not afraid to share.

Second, things always get harder before they can ever get better. I hated when she told me that. I mean, how much harder does it need to get?

But the third thing she taught me was what changed everything. It would be the foundation upon which my life today was built.

"Sweet pea, look around you. There are so many people who love and care about you."

I would get so mad at this, because how dare she think I had time to look around me. I couldn't do anything else but focus on the hell I was experiencing.

Yet, every day we had counseling, she would tell me the same thing. At some point, it clicked. She was not asking me to change my perspective. Really, abuse of any kind was not something you could change your perspective on, especially the things I had faced. She was asking me basically to shift my focus. Once I did that, I would start to learn lessons that helped shape me into who I am today.

T.D. Jakes says there are three types of friends:

1. Constitutes: They are not necessarily loyal to you, personally, but they share allegiance with your mission or your cause. If they meet someone who can further their own cause or goals better than you can, they will leave you.

2. Comrades: They are not for you or your cause but are against what you are against. They will be with you as long as you are both fighting a common enemy. However, they will leave you, once the enemy is defeated.

3. Confidants: These are the most precious of friends. Many of us only have two or three of them over the course of a lifetime. These friendships are marked by their intimacy and level of shared trust, and these people often remain part of our lives for a long time.

Confidants may be described as friends who are there for you, regardless of the situation. They love you unconditionally. They will be a constant in your life and do not leave when difficulties arise.

You can be yourself and do not need to put on a "show" to impress them. With these friends, you can feel comfortable being your authentic self.

Confidants allow you to confide in them and support your dreams, and they are deeply connected to you. These friends will not judge you and will be honest with you, knowing that your friendship can survive the occasional hurt feelings and disappointments.

Michelle is my confidant. My constant. She has remained in my life since the day I met her, when I was fourteen years old and walked through the doors of Anchor House. She has seen me at my best and at my worst. And when I have struggled with understanding things in life, down to the very lows of life. COVID was one of those difficult times.

Many of us who have faced trauma keep busy to distract us from facing things we know we need to face and work through, in order to move forward in the healing process. Man, I didn't realize how many things I was running away from until I had nowhere to run.

And yet, through the craziness she has never left. Always knowing the right way to handle "my" emotions and "my" process for coming to accept things the way they are. Actually, one other lesson she taught me came during this time.

"You can't expect people to be who 'you' want them to be. You have to accept them in your life as they are." My expectations were not where they needed to be.

I am so lucky that she is still in my life today. And while she knows just how much I love her, this can be a little reminder.

I am forever grateful for you. For knowing when to pull me in and when to keep me at an arm's-length away, until I get my grounding. For being the reason that all of the 30-second moments began. For never leaving me when I gave you plenty of opportunity to.

Thank you for teaching me about unconditional love. For teaching me what a safe hug feels like. For teaching me what it feels like to be loved and how to love someone back. And for giving me someone to look up to.

Michelle

A little something else I loved and considered a good childhood memory was the drive to the Alateen meetings. This group was for kids who had addicted parents.

I hated going to the actual meeting, but on our way, we would make two stops. First was McDonald's, to get their fries, and then go over to Burger King, for chocolate milkshakes. Michelle introduced me to dipping your fries in the shake.

Chapter Twelve

Mrs. Komjathy

My favorite teacher during eighth grade was my math teacher, Mrs. Komjathy. No, not because of the subject. I loathe math and have never done well. Something about her drew me in. Well, I guess I know. Again, she checked off some of the mom boxes. Pretty, nice, made me feel safe, and always made me smile.

Mrs. Komjathy wasn't just my teacher. She was also a volunteer at Anchor House. Maybe a coincidence, or maybe how I was referred to Anchor House. So, there I saw my favorite teacher at school and then outside of school.

Once again throwing myself out there with vulnerability, it was sort of the closest thing to a mom figure I would get at that time. Added to that, because Anchor House didn't have transportation to my school, she volunteered to take me.

Every day, I was getting a ride with my favorite teacher. The one whom I wished could rescue me and be my mom. To this day, I wish I could remember those car rides. But they are a blur. I often think, What if I told her? What if I'd said to her the things I had gone through, the things I was still going through, and what it was like living with my mother and family? What if I just had that courage... Would she say she would take me? Sometimes, the what-ifs are a killer.

One day, though, I came the closest I ever have to feeling what I thought a mom would say about "her" child. Someone came to visit her at school that day. I remember this day as if it were right now, as I am typing this.

I was at my locker, which was just across the hall from her classroom. She called me over. She was standing outside of her class door, facing the gentleman who was there to see her.

When I got over to her, she brushed my long, curly hair off my shoulders then placed her hands there and introduced me to him. "This is *my* Denise."

In less than 30 seconds, I went from a kid who was always told no one would ever want them, and who felt the truth in that, to a kid whose favorite teacher had just said, "This is *my* Denise."

But it wasn't the words that had the greatest impact. It was the feeling that I got in those 30 seconds. It was the first time I'd felt "wanted" so deep inside. Or at least I think that is what it feels like to other people.

Anytime I think of that moment, I can feel it as if it is happening all over again. It only took 30 seconds for her to say something to me that made me feel a way I had never felt before, yet it transcended the time it took for her to even say those simple words. Simple and not literally meant. These words and that feeling would be the lifeline I needed to get through each day.

After Anchor House, I was set up to live with my uncle and aunt at the time. My mother didn't want me back, which was okay by me, since I never wanted to go back. The arrangement sounded perfect to me.

Although they didn't live near the school, I was told they would take me every day, so that I could finish out my eighth-grade year. However, that was not the case. I would find out that they planned on switching me to a Catholic school near them.

Not only was I taken away from Anchor House and Michelle, but now I was being taken away from the school where my friends were, the school where I felt safest, and the teacher who actually made me feel wanted. I cannot begin to explain the anger that raged through me.

But what choice did I really have? Within a week of me moving to my aunt and uncle's, it was very clear that their marriage was not good, either. There were daily heated arguments. This was a trigger for me.

After witnessing so many arguments, growing up, that seemed always to lead to physical violence and ultimately me to blame, I started to freak out. I had to come up with a plan. I needed to get back to my old school. Get back to my friends. Get back to my teacher.

I begged my mom (hardest thing I ever did) to let me come stay with her for one weekend. It took some convincing, but she agreed. Every weekend, my mother would go to the Wishy Washy laundromat. So, I planned it out, minute by minute, for how I was going to make my getaway.

After she left for the laundromat, I grabbed my bike and took off. I knew where I would go first, as it had been planned out with my friends, and I knew I had to continue to move, since surely they would be looking for me. Most of the day, I would catch rides out of town then back in town.

Eventually, I was talked into going to one of my ex-Anchor House friend's house. Her mom was a social worker (yeah, I have no idea why she was in Anchor House). They convinced me that she would help me. It was getting pretty late in the day. I had been on the run for hours and, at this point, was starving.

Not long after I got there, two policemen showed up. Yeah, not so helpful after all. I was taken to a place called the Youth Emergency Center, which was located in a hospital. (That program has since been disbanded.) This was the hospital where my mother had been admitted into the psych ward a few times.

They took me to a room and sat me at a table. The only thing I remember is some fat guy coming in and sitting across from me. His words are still searing to this day.

He pushed a plain piece of paper and a pen over in front of me. Then, he said, "You have two choices. You could either write down how you made all of this up, so you could get attention. *Or* you can be admitted into the psych ward."

I kid you not, that was exactly what he told me. He said that my mother was in the process of filling out the forms, because she said I was mentally ill and needed help. But somehow it was said that, if I would just write down and sign a statement that I was making everything up, she would take me back with her.

I remember sitting there for a few minutes. I was angry. I felt defeated. I was dying inside. Maybe, I thought, if I just got admitted, I would get medicated enough to have the courage to say something, no matter if I was wrong or not.

But if I signed, what would all those teachers, *that* teacher, think of me?

I was so hungry that, at that point all I wanted to do was get a Whopper Junior with cheese, fries, and a milkshake from Burger King. And I knew it would also be the only way I could get back to my old school, to see my friends and see my teacher.

Things would go back to the way they were prior to Anchor House, but now with that signed paper being held over my head by my mother. All I could do to get through each day was look forward to seeing my favorite teacher.

Each day, when my mother would scream at me, telling me she hated me or wished I was someone else, I would think about that 30-second moment I'd gotten from Mrs. Komjathy and remind myself of that feeling. Even when my mom hit me, I could go back to that moment and disappear in my head from what was happening to me.

I even went to bed at night reliving the moment, just so I could fall asleep. I realized that those 30 seconds had had more of an impact on me than other big things that had happened in my life. At no other time did I have a feeling that hit me so deep inside. This would be the beginning of the 30-second moments.

During the summer between eighth grade and high school, I was involved in a car accident. I had told my mother I was staying somewhere else, so this place was not where I was supposed to be. After I got into the ambulance, they asked for my parents' number. My best friend at the time was in the ambulance with me, and she knew what would happen if they called my mother.

I remembered, in my yearbook, Mrs. Komjathy had written, "If you ever need me, you know where to find me." I had looked up her number, in case I got the courage to use my voice.

My friend knew this and gave them her number, but, of course, she said she couldn't help. Then, they tried Anchor House again, with no luck. Ultimately, my mother was called, and, well, let's just say things never changed.

However, after that, I was so embarrassed that I had given them Mrs. Komjathy's number. I felt like she must now believe my mother, that I was the problem. I never went back to see her until a few years ago.

Recently, I saw her over the summer. I was able to let her know how she made an impact on my life and that she helped me be the mom I am today. But I didn't have the opportunity to really tell her why.

If I had the chance to see her again and had a few minutes to spend, I would tell her this....

Thank You. I don't think I could properly put into words what you have meant to me.

You helped me to feel safe when most of my days were spent in fear of the unknown. You found the good things in me when most would only see the bad. You made me feel like I was special and important, when every day at home I was not.

And in that innocent 30-second moment, when you referred to me as "my Denise," you taught me what it feels like to be wanted. Every kid wants to be wanted.

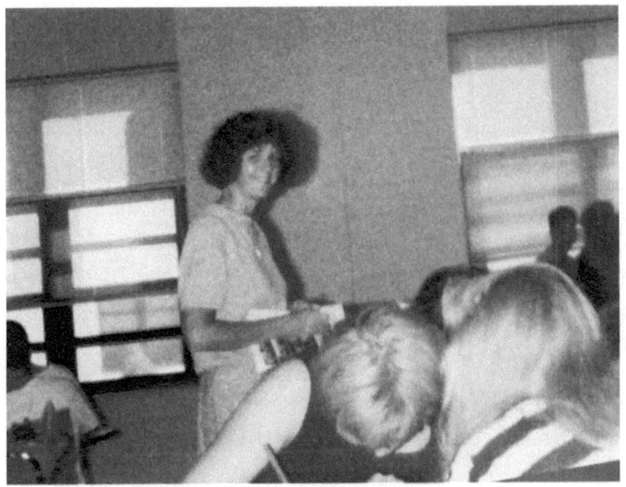

Mrs. Komjathy

Chapter Thirteen

Mrs. Pasko

This is a short chapter but one I did not want to miss including. Another teacher whom I should mention from that time was a teacher I went from being afraid of to actually liking. She was my history teacher, Mrs. Pasko.

She was one of those teachers who looked mean (sorry, Mrs. Pasko). She was a very disciplined teacher, where there was no horsing around allowed or pulling any nonsense. Ms. Pasko was straightforward. Even me, the kid who argued with anyone and didn't care, actually cared not to get into too much trouble in her history class. That's not to say I didn't run my mouth a time or two. Actually, I used to wonder how far I could push it before she would give up on me. She never really did.

I went into Anchor House in late October, right before Halloween. One day just prior, she called me over to her desk after everyone had left class. I thought for sure I must have done something wrong and was about to get into trouble.

Instead, she asked, if she could get permission, would I want to come home with her and trick-or-treat with her kids?

Ugh. My fight-or-flight kicked in. Heart pounding and terrified I would screw something up if I went, I politely declined. I'll never forget that day, though, or how she made me feel. She looked past my "fighting" persona and saw me, the fourteen-year-old kid who was facing so many challenges. This is another decision that eats me alive today. I just wish I'd had the courage to say yes and go.

If I had the chance to tell her, I would want her to know this...

The lesson you taught me was to look beyond what you see on the outside and see the person on the inside. We all want to be seen.

Mrs. E. Pasko

Chapter Fourteen

Patty

As my eighth-grade year ended, so did my ability to look forward to the next day, since I would no longer see my favorite teacher.

That summer was difficult. We again were changing schools, going from middle school to high school, where some of my middle-school group of friends would not be around.

My elementary-school best friends were my saving grace during summer breaks and holidays. I would spend as much time as I could at their houses. They were my safe place.

While I was still close with my elementary-school best friends, we ventured out like most friend groups do, as you change schools. That year, I decided to head into playing soccer again. I wasn't a great soccer player, but I like to think I could hold my own.

Each of us went to high school trying new things. Salina went into track, Sandy to color guard, and me back to playing soccer. I wasn't a great soccer player, but I'd like to think I could hold my own.

That year there was only a varsity team. Back in the late eighties and early nineties, girls' soccer wasn't what it is like today. Actually, it wasn't until my sophomore year when more and more girls came out to play. So, freshman year, we had two coaches, Patty and Lisa. Patty was actually the wife of one of the eighth-grade gym teachers.

He wasn't my teacher, but he was one who knew me. I had thought for sure he must have told Patty about me and my situation. Years later, she said she never knew, or at least that's what she said to me.

So, I was hesitant at first. I was still a little lippy, but that wouldn't last too long. I grew to really admire her. She was like that big sister you always wanted to hang with and hoped would look out for you.

In the beginning, I wasn't sure if I was going to make it on this team. Not that I would be cut, because at that time they really didn't cut anyone who wanted to play. I mean that I was dying, trying to run.

She pushed me to limits I didn't think I could survive. So many days doing suicide drills (relay running, back and forth, sideline to sideline), when I would always end up being the last one back and have to repeat them until I threw up. Gatorade going down is great, but coming up, it was not.

But, at each practice, I found myself being able to do more than I'd done before.

Off the field, I was still getting into fights. Because, after returning home to my mother's, I went back to being the person who would fight anyone for someone else. Not the smartest thing, but I was full of rage and anger.

I would still mouth off to the occasional teacher. However, not enough to get into serious trouble. All of the fistfights were off school grounds. But one day, my mouth got me into a bit of trouble with my coach.

She must have said something that I didn't like, and I snipped right back. I still remember her head whipping around and her looking dead at me. "You run your mouth again, and you can take a seat on that bench."

Holy shit! I was not prepared for that at all. She would later tell the team, if we got into trouble at school or got a failing grade, we would be sitting the bench and not playing. Well, that was all I needed to hear.

Soccer became like the detention I used to get all the time in middle school. It was what kept me from having to go home. The more I played, the more I really looked up to coach. Again, I wasn't the best, but she never gave up on me and continued to push me to do more than I ever thought I could.

Fall came, and soccer ended. Patty was not only the soccer coach, but she was also the freshmen basketball coach. She strongly encouraged her freshman soccer players to play basketball. Now, I am five feet tall. Some would argue that I'm 4'11". There is nothing about me that screams basketball player. But just as in soccer, she pushed me to do things I didn't think I could do.

She became the reason I looked forward to the next day. As much as I dreaded drills, I couldn't wait to go to practice. I should mention, my basketball skills were not impressive and would not improve enough to play a second year. But that is another story.

During that time, I had made friends with a group of girls who came from "normal" homes. I was desperately trying to fit in with people with whom I would never fit in, yet I still tried. A few of us had Patty for soccer and a couple of girls just met her during basketball. Our group of friends all seemed to want Patty's attention.

I continued to try to build my friendships with this group of girls. I was always feeling on the outside but determined to somehow make it work. Now, normally, I would never have anyone come to my house. Especially when we were living in a one-bedroom apartment. Yet for some reason, one night, I had a sleepover. I had never had a sleepover outside of with my elementary school best friends and only because they knew what my situation was and would always be the first to protect me, when they could.

I remember the night the girls came over. We had to pull the couch bed out, which is where we all tried to fit, to sleep. Back in the early nineties, there weren't cell phones to take video. Instead, we had these big cameras with VHS cassette tapes.

We were videoing when one of the girls pushed me while I had orange juice in my hands, and it went all over. I cannot begin to tell you the sheer panic that came over me. I was praying to God my mother wouldn't explode while they were there.

I did everything to clean up as quickly as I could because she was just in the bedroom, watching TV. I managed to make it look like nothing had happened. The night went on, and that was that. No more sleepovers or people coming to my house. After that, we would sleep at one of their houses.

During the sleepovers at their house, things were so much different than at mine. The parents were always there, and they always had snacks and pizza. It was not what I was used to.

And at night, they would talk about their diaries. *Diaries*? Oh, hell no. I do not write anything down. Ever since that fat man told me to write that I'd made things up, I no longer documented anything. I knew better. But I really wanted to fit in. So, I bought one. With a key!

Basketball was going okay, but the friends group was a little rocky. Teen girls are teen girls and very gossipy about one another. One girl and I were definitely not made to be friends. But I tried.

There was this constant competition for who Patty liked better. It was ridiculous. I found myself writing about this, as well as other things. I started to write more than I should, thinking I didn't have to worry about my mother reading it, since I had a key.

In this book, I wrote about Anchor House, about some of the things my mother did and would do. About how I wished all these other women could be my mom. Oh, that was one thing that should never, and I mean *never* have been written in ink, or written at all for that matter.

Christmas break rolled around. No school to go to, and no basketball practice. Most kids like me would dread this time of the year. Or any time we had off, really. There was no escape. No safe place. You were again facing battles that beat you till you feel you can't go anymore. During this break, my mother came across that diary.

One day, after we got to the laundromat, she whipped it out and began to read it aloud for everyone—and I mean everyone—to hear. She chose to read every part that described whom I wished I could have for a mom.

Then, she began screaming that I was an ungrateful brat. That she gave me everything. She continued to read aloud more and more.

All I could do was sit there in embarrassment. My stomach felt like it was twisting inside out. I couldn't run, and there was nowhere to hide. What made it worse was that the owner of the laundromat was one of the women I'd "wished was my mom." However, she didn't read that part aloud, either because she hadn't gotten to it, or she wouldn't say it.

Finally, school started again and so did basketball practice. Something that gave me the only will to go on another day. However, I was on the brink, and something said by one of the friends pushed me to be defeated.

I was made to believe that maybe I was too much for the coach, just as I was for everyone else who left me. It was my abandonment issues coming into play.

With no one left to help me look forward to the next day, I once again planned out my ending. However, this time, I did not care if anyone claimed to be the victim. I was so done.

I woke up the next day and decided I would go to practice one last time. As I was walking in, Patty, our coach, came walking alongside me, threw her arm around me and pulled me into a headlock, all while saying, "I think I'm gonna take you under my wing."

Time stopped. Everything in me froze, except I could hear Michelle's voice saying, "There are people who care about you."

In that 30-second moment, I felt like I mattered to someone. Someone who I had wished could rescue me, who actually did rescue me. She gave me the will to live another day and days after that. In less than 30 seconds, Patty saved my life.

I stayed friendly with a few girls but ultimately pulled away from being "part" of the group. I never really did feel like I fit in anywhere. I spent too much time just trying to survive. I always maintained my close friendship with the sisters, but as we got older, we, too, expanded to find more friends.

The next fall came, and soccer was back on. Every day, I looked forward to the dreaded practice or game, always making sure I never had my family come to see us. I had to keep my two worlds separate. It was the only way for me to survive. I was always afraid that my mother and grandmother would gang up and push the positive people out of my life.

Winter sports came, but this time I would not make it on the basketball team. I wasn't totally surprised. I knew I was not good or remotely decent at playing basketball. So, of course, panic set in. Now what?

I knew the only thing that kept me going was having something to look forward to the next day.

It would be almost a year before I would have soccer. And we would find out that Patty would not be returning. She was starting a family. To say I wasn't a bit crushed would be a lie. But at least it wasn't something that I'd done.

Today, I call Patty my friend. It was only a few years ago when we connected through an Anchor House ride that she participates in every year, raising money for the Anchor House Foundation which helps Anchor House.

In 2018, I was invited to speak at the fortieth anniversary of Anchor House. There, I not only was able to speak about the significance Anchor House had had on my life, but also able to show how it led me to recognize the genuine care Patty had for me, which ultimately saved my life that day she took me in that headlock.

So, while I have shared how thankful I was during that dinner, here is a reminder:

Thank you for teaching me how to see something in someone that they don't see in themselves.

Teaching me what it feels like to matter. And, as I have been able to share with you before, thank you for saving my life.

Patty

Chapter Fifteen

Mrs. Sedia

After being cut from the basketball team, I wasn't sure what I was going to do. But I realized that I really did have someone else who had been right in front of me the whole time. I was so focused on the relationship with my coach, I just didn't notice.

I don't remember how the connection happened between Mrs. Sedia and me, other than she was my teacher. Well, maybe I should say that I do remember. If I'm being honest, I was still hoping for a rescue from a "mother" figure, and she definitely checked off all the boxes.

There was something about her that made it so easy to talk to her. She had a very approachable personality and became the person I looked forward to seeing, day after day. She was the reason I got up and showed up to school.

She didn't know anything about my background. I was just like any other student, as far as she knew. We had a kindred spirit. We had some very relatable stories from our childhoods. Maybe that is what made it easy.

I remember the first day when I went to sit in the car to talk to her. That was back when it was an okay thing to do. Mrs. Sedia turned toward me and then tapped me on the knee, while asking, "Okay, so tell me, what's going on? How are you?"

In less than 30 seconds, I went from being just a kid who was told and made to feel not worthy to a kid who felt that I was worth someone else's time. She wanted to be there as much as I needed to be there.

I think the relationship, from that day forward, just grew. It was like she could read me and know when I needed to talk or just sit while she talked. I'd walk down the hall, and she would give me a look and say, "Come see me after school."

I still kept quiet about the truth. I still held onto the secrets for fear she would not believe me or for fear she would just tell me how "normal" it was.

There were so many moments when I would tell myself that I could do it. Just tell her. But each time, that pounding in my heart started, and I would try and find a way out. It was like fight-or-flight.

No matter how much I wanted to be "rescued," I would still find myself terrified at telling someone and actually being "rescued." I didn't know how to survive "being safe." That sounds ridiculous, but the truth is there are many of us who feel that way. We learn how to live in the chaos, so anything remotely "normal" makes the flight mode kick in. It is a frustrating feeling to get, when you have spent your whole life wishing for something different.

One of those times came after one night, while I was working at a place called Cluck You Chicken. It was a fast-food wing place just next door to the apartment where I lived. I started working there in eleventh grade, when my grandmother told me I needed to give my mother money to "help her out."

One night, I had a late shift. It wasn't like I had never worked on a school night or had a curfew or a bedtime. But something triggered my mother.

She came into the pickup line, screaming at me. I was walking out to the parking lot to give someone their food, and when I turned around, she was yelling in my face.

Out of nowhere, I said, "Fuck you." It was so quick, I literally didn't know what hit me.

Well, I mean, I did—it was her hand. But I was still in shock. I should have said it again and again, so she would continue to hit me. Maybe she would have gotten arrested, because there were witnesses. Maybe, then, I would have had the courage.

I don't know how it ended. I do remember walking back in and everyone asking if I was okay.

One of the girls who was with me at Anchor House also worked with me at the restaurant. The one whose mother was a shitty social worker who'd turned me in to the police, when I ran away. I remember begging her not to say a word. I can't believe she actually listened. The marks that were left were faint enough to cover with makeup.

And the name of that wing place, Cluck You Chicken, would get the nickname Clock You Chicken by those who saw what happened. Honestly, I laugh now. Sometimes, you need to find the humor in things.

My thoughts quickly shifted to survival. As with all of my 30-second moments, I would relive them in my head, as if they were all happening right then and there, so that I would be able to get through the weight of what was happening. Maybe I would tell Mrs. Sedia the next day. Maybe, this time, I could do it. But, I didn't. I kept quiet, like I always did.

At this point, there was no hope left for me. All hope for me was gone when I turned sixteen. I knew then that there would be no rescue. No way out of the hell I was living. There would be no "mom." There would be no safe place.

Now, when I was seventeen, there was even less hope. No one wants a seventeen-year-old. So, all I could do was survive. Those moments talking with Mrs. Sedia were what kept me going.

Although they were simple moments, they were my lifeline. And she would always show up.

I would tell her about a soccer game, and she would show up on the sidelines. I would tell her about the plays I was in at the local college, and she would show up in the audience. Again, the closest I would get to having a mom. Sometimes, you need to look around and find the people who care about you.

I reconnected with Mrs. Sedia the year I was getting married. And just like she did before, she showed up to the church. My husband, who was in the Air Force, was transferred to another state right after we got married. Still, I kept in touch with her.

A few years later, we would temporarily move back to New Jersey, and Mrs. Sedia continued to be there for me. Through the times when my youngest was sick in the hospital to the time when I needed help with my house. She recruited her husband, whom I'd also had as a teacher, and he too would show up for me.

A little story about Mr. Sedia. He actually knew all about my family. I am not sure he ever told Mrs. Sedia when I was back in high school. He knew secrets that even I didn't know. I never had to explain myself to him; he just got it. He always knew the right words to say to support me.

Growing up, facing what I had faced, I never trusted men. But I wasn't afraid of him. There were never ulterior motives. There were times when I would just talk to him and get the rough-and-gruff advice. I seriously loved the sprinkle of curse words he chose to use in our conversations. I do it myself, which made the conversations even better.

Mr. Sedia passed away in late 2022. I stared in disbelief when Mrs. Sedia told me. Because of how I lived growing up, I never cried in front of people. My grandmother had passed earlier that year, and I didn't cry once. But this one was different.

I will miss his smirk and laugh, when I would tell him the current gossip I'd heard about my family. Or how he would say those two words, which I can still hear, "F**k em," and "Who cares what they think?" I find myself still hearing those words often.

Years ago, when I was struggling with something, he gave me a card he kept in his wallet. It was the Serenity Prayer. I have carried that in my own wallet ever since that day.

A classmate who writes a sports column in a paper wrote about Mr. Sedia, after he passed. He wrote, "Mr. Sedia always rooted for the underdog." And an underdog I was.

You may be wondering why, as an adult, I don't call them by their first names. To me, it is like calling your parents by their first name. I've never been comfortable calling them Barbara or Bob. To me, they will always be Mr. and Mrs. Sedia.

While she knows how much she means to me, I also want her to know how thankful I am for teaching me more than just a subject in school.

Thank you for teaching me all about empathy, compassion, and kindness. For teaching me how to listen. How we can't always fix the broken, but we can always be there to validate someone's feelings. For teaching me how to show up as you always showed up for me and how worthy that can make someone feel. Thank you for believing in me.

Mrs. Sedia

Chapter Sixteen

North Carolina

During the summer between my junior and senior year, I had two kids knock on my door. When I opened it up, there was a teen boy and girl, and they said they were my cousins.

What? I had never seen them before. Come to find out, they were my biological dad's cousins.

My paternal side of the family was missing throughout most of my childhood. Outside of his dad and new wife, who, I will admit, did come to visit me, no one else was there. And when I went to Anchor House, my mother must have told them that I was mentally ill, because they never came back.

The cousins told me the story of what they'd been told, which was all fake, that my great-grandmother had hired a detective to find me. I'll admit she was a wealthy woman, but I am certain it didn't take a detective. I soon became very close with my two cousins.

A short time after meeting them, I went to meet my great-grandmother and her husband. MeMe and Pop was what the kids called them. They lived in a historic home in Princeton—well, right outside, but close enough.

I remember one night, my cousin K and I slept over, and she told me all the "hauntings" that had happened there. Now, I am not one for scary movies, so hauntings were nothing I wanted to take part in.

During one of the visits, there was a couple with their two small children whom I was introduced to. They, too, were cousins but distant. They lived in North Carolina and lived a somewhat "normal" life. MeMe arranged for K and me to fly down and spend a week there. This was so out of my comfort zone. Remember, I only knew how to live in the world of chaos, not in the "normal" world.

During this time, I really got a full inside peek at what a "normal" family was like. I know, no one is normal. And yes, that would soon come to light. But, for the time being, it was a world I had only peeked through the windows to see.

Dana again checked off all the mom boxes. Staying there for two weeks was honestly the closest I had ever come in my life to that lived experience. She was the type of mom I'd envisioned.

She loved spending time with her kids. Every meal was eaten together as a family, except, of course, for lunch, when her husband, Greg, was working. Let me just tell you, he was one of the funniest guys I had ever met. Also, one of only two men I trusted to be around. I looked at both of them as what I wished for in parents.

The first night we were there, we all sat down for dinner. I went to pick up my fork to eat when, all of a sudden, they said, "Let's pray," and grabbed hands. Right as I was picking up the fork and before they grabbed hands, my cousin K kicked me under the table, to stop me from digging in. I laugh thinking about that.

Our week there was great, in my book. Greg took us to see James Taylor at the Hardee's Center. I had never been to a concert, although this was a small one and at an outdoor amphitheater.

We helped Dana in the kitchen and watched the kids, not as chores but more as a family. Again, this was from my perspective. I just remember soaking everything in. There was a comfort in having K there with me.

It soon came to an end and we had to fly back to New Jersey. I had such a hard time. I didn't want to go back home.

About a week later, Dana and Greg made arrangements for me to come back. K didn't want to go, so I was going to be doing this alone. Instead of flying, though, I would be taking a train. The deal was I would have to spend the rest of the summer there. I was all for it until I wasn't.

It was definitely a bit harder for me without having K with me. I think there was a comfort in having someone else who didn't have this lifestyle. I was also very close to K, so leaving her was hard.

I can't remember when it happened, but I do remember my reaction. They had a basketball hoop in their driveway. Again, I was not great at basketball, but I will say there were some calming factors about taking all those shots with no one around.

While I was outside, Greg came out to shoot some hoops. Now, I have to tell you, I saw Greg as a dad figure. Most men scared me, but he was how I pictured having a dad would be.

We were out there for a few minutes when Dana opened the door and called out to him. Something happened that caused them to argue. Right away, my fight-or-flight kicked in. I was flying.

I'd grown up being told I was the reason for things that went wrong. So, clearly, I assumed that their argument was something I'd done.

While he went into the house, I just sat behind the car in the driveway, trying to figure out how I could get back to the chaos I knew how to survive back at home. Long story short, I came up with a plan and got home. But I remained very grateful for the time I spent there at their home.

I left having learned two things. One was what it felt like to be in a good "home." (I really did look at you like the mom and dad I didn't have.) And two, for helping me see the mom I wanted to be like someday.

Dana

Chapter Seventeen

Senior Year

I returned home to New Jersey to the chaos of what my life had always been. I never really found the place where I felt I fit in or where I felt I really belonged. When I look back at pictures of high school, I don't look back and see great times. Instead, I look back and see the kid who was just trying to silently survive.

I had been told for years that, when I turned eighteen, I would have to leave. But I was still in high school because of staying back. Things continued as they had always done. But now, I was a legal adult.

What does that mean? Well, it meant that all—and I mean *all*—hope for any type of rescue to get me out of that environment was gone. It also meant that the fear of Child Protective Services being called was no longer an issue. It meant I was now officially alone in the chaos of life.

I think I went to sit in Mrs. Sedia's car on a daily basis, or that's what it felt I did. Even after turning eighteen, I still could not muster up the courage to tell her what had happened to me or how I was still being treated.

One day, I was on the phone with my cousin K, and something triggered my mother. She came into the room, grabbed the phone, and started to swing it at me. All I could do was laugh, while shouting out to my cousin that I had to call her back.

I get a lot of people who ask, "How can you laugh at something like that?" Well, when you grow up with these types of things as your "normal," you learn that crying gets you nowhere. They say "laughter is the best medicine."

Senior year was another time when I took off, only to return on my own the next day. During senior year, I also returned to finding the numbness in parties on the weekends.

During this year, I started to work at a restaurant. I made a great group of friends, where I finally felt I could fit in, even in the chaos of my life. There were so many memories made. I was mostly the only girl. I found having male friends easier than females. There wasn't the cattiness that comes with female friendships.

One summer weekend, my friend's parents left town, and of course that meant it was a two-night party. The only thing I remember eating was Chicken Alfredo, which was to help soak up the countless cups of vodka and orange juice. I just remember it being a great time.

That time, though, would also be when I had a wake-up call. At another party, I drank a pitcher full of vodka and orange juice and ended up having my stomach pumped. I didn't take a drink after that until I turned twenty-one.

All through those times, I played out the 30-second moments. Without the escape to school or seeing my teachers, I didn't have anything else to help me through. And within those 30-second moments came the realization that I wanted those teachers to see me someday and be proud, not disappointed. I never knew the significance of this till I had my own children.

Chapter Eighteen

After High School

After high school, I went to community college. While I did get into some universities, I didn't have the money or the guidance to help pay the tuition. Just another reminder that I didn't have the mom I'd wished for who would help steer me the right way.

I only made it through a semester and a half at the county college. I was unable to handle working full-time to pay rent and going full-time to college. So, I quit.

I also started to see a therapist. Against the wishes of my mother and grandmother, but I was paying for it, and I was an "adult." I saw her for two years. This was the first therapist I had seen outside of Anchor House and the school counselors.

In my two years of opening up about some of the things I had never shared before, two things came out that stand in my mind today. One, I told her that I never thought I would live to see twenty-one. I thought for sure I would be dead.

The second thing was something she said. She told me that the best thing for me to do would be to walk away from my family and cut my mother out.

I told her I was afraid. And I felt sorry. *Ugh,* that last one. I felt bad for her, because someone needed to be able to help defend her from my grandmother and whomever else she needed protection from. Someone was always after her. (That is what she believed and what she would convince me of).

One time, I had to pull her out of a car window she'd jumped into to beat up some woman who'd made remarks about a boyfriend, while the sounds of sirens came closer. I'd been in my teens. So, my excuse for not leaving was that no one would do that for her. Once again, I was not thinking of myself, because I was trapped in the fear of what other people would think of me. But I would learn, eventually, that the advice my therapist gave me was the one thing that freed me.

In my early twenties, I was still trying to figure out where I belonged. As most of us do, I made some good choices and some bad choices. Just part of growing up.

Chaos and abuse still played out within the family. The abuse changed as I grew. One thing stayed the same, though: the back-and-forth chess game between my grandmother and mother. Everyone wanted you to take a side. And should I not take either side, they, of course, came together as a team to shut me down.

Silently, I continued to use my survival and coping skills. I reminded myself of the impactful moments with all the women in my past. I reminded myself of the lessons I'd learned. I reminded myself that I wanted to make them "proud," if ever I saw them again. Your survival and coping skills never go away. I believe they grow with us, as we grow older.

During the podcast with Ann, we discovered something else we had in common. During my twenties, I was still hoping for a "mom." I knew it wasn't going to happen, but that was part of my survival. I think it is safe to say there are more of us out there who felt this way, going into our adult lives. It isn't talked about, so it feels very isolating.

Now in my forties, I no longer "search" for a mom. But there are still parts of me that wish someone would come out of the woodwork and say, "I wanted to take you," "I would have loved to take you," "I never stopped thinking about you."

Not because I am looking for a "mom" relationship anymore. That time has come and gone. Now, all I can hope is to know that, somewhere out there, someone thought of me.

I think there are a lot of us who feel that way, we just don't tell anyone. Unless you have ever felt being overlooked, unseen, unheard, unwanted, or have been without a "mom" or family, you really wouldn't get it.

That's why most of us keep silent as adults. We are ashamed and embarrassed for having those thoughts.

Chapter Nineteen

Moving Away

I met my husband when I was twenty-four. We got married ten months later and have been married now for twenty-three years. Sitting in the church during our wedding were two of the women who made a great impact in my life: Michelle and Mrs. Sedia. When I tell you Michelle has been there for everything, I mean *everything* — except childbirth, although I am sure she would have come, if I'd asked.

My husband was active duty in the Air Force, and right after we got married, we moved out of state. This was the beginning of what would eventually be the courage I needed to cut off my family.

Over the next two years, we had our two children. First, our daughter, and then, twenty-two months later, our son. Both times, I would not allow my mother or grandmother to come.

For two years, I managed through the trials of being a new mom and not having someone to really call, when I was not sure what to do. I relied on friends, like most of us who have faced an abusive childhood, while we navigate a world that we never thought we would see.

When my son turned a year old, we moved back to New Jersey, while my husband was deployed. It was a move I was somewhat happy for, but at the same time felt so much anxiety over.

I was able to reconnect with a few of the women from my childhood. And just like those 30-second moments that happened while I was younger, I was reminded of the lessons I'd learned from each woman I connected with. I began to recognize that I did not want my kids to witness the chaos I'd had, when I was growing up. But sure enough, things started to creep into my happy little family.

The first red flag was just a week or two after moving back. The kids and I were at my mother's house. I had my son in one arm and my daughter right next to me, when my mother said, "You need to come to my therapy appointment."

Uh, no, I don't.

After saying that I was not coming, she started getting louder and louder. And I kid you not, the words that came out of her mouth were these: "I gave you a cookie-cutter life."

At that moment, I realized I needed to be brave and leave that house. While my husband was deployed, the kids and I were temporarily staying there, while we waited for our furniture to make the move back to New Jersey. After my mother left to go wherever it was she went to, I did what I had done so many years earlier. I calculated the time it would take for me to gather our things and leave.

I took my kids and myself to my biological father's house. I know I haven't talked about him in the book. I'd never stayed with him before. I don't really think I spent that much time with him prior to that day. But I needed to do whatever I could to protect my kids. And it was only for a very short time.

I don't have too much to say about my biological father. He was not in my life, as a kid. I remember seeing him a total of two times. Once was when I was four or five years old, when my mother was "getting back together" with him.

I don't remember seeing him after that day until I was around eight. He had come to visit me at my grandmother's house. She had custody of me at that time. The only thing I remember about that visit was we went into the kitchen, and I felt very uncomfortable. I don't remember what we talked about, except for one thing.

He had asked me to call him a "f**king asshole." Yes, I typed that right. As an adult, the only thing I could come up with is that having me call him that made it easier for him to leave.

If there is one good thing I can say about him, it is that he has never made excuses for his behavior. He has owned up to his wrongs, which I respect him for doing.

We had a decent relationship during the six years we lived in New Jersey. It wasn't really a father-daughter relationship. I am not quite sure what I would call it. Maybe just two adults who happen to be biologically related, I guess.

I respected him, and he respected me. There were times when I felt that uneasy feeling, mostly when he was drinking. My father was a functioning alcoholic. We don't have a real relationship any more. Just an occasional text here and there.

Chapter Twenty

Finding Courage

After an extended stay in New Jersey of six years, we were finally moving out of state. And this would prove to be the move that I needed to happen. While I was still wrestling with the outcome that would eventually come, I had to make the decision to protect my kids.

In 2014, I sat on the floor, holding my son after his seizure, when I started getting text notifications. It was my mother. Text after text telling me that I was a sick person, that everyone was talking about me. About how she gave me a cookie-cutter life and that no one in the family wanted anything to do with me, because of how sick in the head that I was, all the while cursing me out.

And as I sat there, looking at my son, I took the phone and hit the block button. Just like that.

What followed was exactly what she had told me my whole life. Almost all of my family stopped talking to me. The people whom I never wanted to push away now believed every word she said about me. All I wanted to do was to scream the truth, looking for validation. But what I eventually learned was that validation will never erase the nightmares or the pain. So, I stopped looking for it.

It was time for me to focus on my own life with my kids and my husband. I had to learn not to be afraid every time the phone rang or the mail came. I had spent my whole life walking on eggshells, never knowing what would happen. What would trigger an outrage. I would have to learn how to relax in a safe environment.

That sounds so crazy, saying that as an adult, but it was true. Just like when I was a kid and wanted to be rescued but was also scared of it, because I didn't know how to "be" in a safe environment. I would have to learn to just be me.

My focus turned to my kids and making sure that they felt safe, wanted, happy, and loved. One of the things I worried about was... how? How do I make sure they have those feelings? Well, I had to think back to the women who'd showed me how to make someone feel safe, wanted, happy, and loved.

My kids never asked about my mother or other family members. (My youngest has autism, so he really never noticed.) I think because we were no longer in the state and they were so busy playing with the kids in the neighborhood and being adjusted to the military moves, it made the old family fade away.

In the beginning, any time my daughter would ask about any family member, which really was not but a handful of times, initially, I told her that that person had moved and we hadn't gotten their number yet. I never once talked negatively about any of them. I didn't want my kids to grow up playing the chess game.

Over the course of the next three years, my mother would send cards with her phone number to the kids, asking them to call her. They were only seven and eight when that began, so of course, we didn't give them the cards.

After her attempts with the cards were unsuccessful, she reached out to the teachers who were still in my life. Mrs. Sedia told me a few years later how she'd called her twice, trying to get her to think I was crazy.

My mother was desperate to force contact. In 2017, I received a call from *The Dr. Phil Show*. They asked if I would come on with her.

After I declined, my mother then called social services, claiming I had made my children ill. Both of my kids have genetic disorders that they inherited from me (the belief is, because I was exposed in utero to the drugs and alcohol, I passed on defects). The case was closed quickly, as all of the doctors and specialists provided proof of the genetics.

A few years later, things would again escalate, but this time for the worst. This time, I went to a judge and asked for a protection order.

My mother began texting my daughter's email. This bypassed her number being blocked, since it came in as an email. (Honestly, I don't know how she got her email address). In one of her texts to my daughter, she said, "What goes around comes around."

This was a trigger for me. When I was in grade school, my mother tried to kidnap me while I was outside playing. She didn't have custody at that time. The judge asked if I was worried that she would do that again, I said yes!

While the judge wouldn't grant a protection order, because it is only good for two years, she proposed and granted a no-contact order, which has no end date.

My mother told the judge that she would agree to it, because her grandchildren would be eighteen soon.

Yeah, that happened. Even the judge was stunned. It was the first time that the courts heard my voice.

Chapter Twenty-One

2020

Like for most people, this was a difficult time for me and my family. For the obvious reasons, as we all felt the isolation. But for me, it was hitting rock-bottom.

As I mentioned before, most of us who have faced trauma tend to keep ourselves busy. Always doing something, so the things we really need to face and learn to heal from never surface long enough for us to confront them. I didn't know how much I was about to face until I had nowhere to run.

I can honestly say I felt like I wanted to turn the lights out. Now, I never would, because of my kids, but I was feeling that same suffocation I felt when I was a kid. I was suffocating from the loneliness. While yes, I had my family right beside me, the internal me was slowly sinking.

Some of the hurt feelings of the fourteen-year-old me resurfaced and made me face the fact that I really hadn't grown up or, rather, healed from that time. (Okay, I am not a huge fan of the word *healed,* because I feel like it means something that will never have to be felt again, which is not truthful.)

One of my closest friends is one of my childhood teachers. Catherine is more like an older sister. She was actually the only person who came to visit me when I lived at Anchor House. So, she knows a lot about my childhood.

One day, we were talking about something that had happened when I was fourteen, and about halfway into the conversation, she stopped me.

She said, "Denise, when you are talking about this time, you sound like you are fourteen. You are not fourteen anymore."

Man, was that eye-opening. I started to listen to myself when we talked, and she was right. I was thrown back in time. What she said had a profound impact and was the thing that would catapult me into facing the things I was not ready to face.

Every time I had gone back, I was once again looking for someone to rescue me. I was looking for someone to reach out to me. I was feeling the fourteen-year-old's hurt from wanting a "mom" to heal me. I was still inside searching for the "mom" I wished I had had, when I was a kid.

All of this was going on internally. It was time for me to "grow up" and learn that I am the only one who can rescue me. That is a hard thing to learn and accept. But it was something that would, again, catapult me to where I am today.

Chapter Twenty-Two

2021

Fast forward to 2021. It was December, and my daughter was turning eighteen. All she had talked about was wanting to take a trip up to New York City for the day.

Up until then, anytime she would ask me about my childhood, I would just say that it wasn't a very good one. I told her, when she turned eighteen, she could ask me anything. So, there we were, driving up to New York, and she started to ask me questions.

So, I told her everything I was comfortable sharing at that time. During the conversation, I talked about Val, Michelle, Ms. Komjathy, Patty, Dana, and Mrs. Sedia. As I finished telling the story, I said to her that I wished I'd had a mom, so I could be a better mom to her.

Without hesitation, she leaned over and put her hand on my arm. She said, "Mom, I am so happy that 'they' raised you, because I love the way you raised me." She said she has always felt safe, has always felt unconditionally loved, has always felt wanted, has always felt that she matters and has always felt that she was worthy of my attention and my time.

For years, people would say to me, "Give them what you wished you'd had." The problem that I had and would get angry about was how could I give them something that I'd never had before? How can you give something that you don't know how to give? Yet here I was the whole time, giving the 30-second moments to my kids.

These simple 30-second moments not only helped "raise" me, but they have also helped me to raise my kids. They taught me everything that I should have been taught at home.

Within those simple moments, the legacy of that babysitter, the counselors, the coach, and every teacher who gave me a simple moment of hope had now transcended the time it actually took for them to say something to me.

30-Second Moments

It only takes 30 seconds.

It only takes 30 seconds for a child to feel safe.

It only takes 30 seconds for a child to feel unconditionally loved.

It only takes 30 seconds for a child to feel wanted.

It only takes 30 seconds for a child to feel seen.

It only takes 30 seconds for a child to feel like they matter.

It only takes 30 seconds for a child to feel worthy.

Every day we are presented with moments of opportunity.

Every day, we may say something to a child that might not mean anything to us, but for that kid, it will be the glimmer of hope they need to get through the day.

You might never know who you are raising. But if you are lucky, one day, someone like me will come back to tell you how you made them feel.

You are the light in the darkness. The beacon of hope. Your legacy lives on in the light.

"People will forget what you said,
People will forget what you did,
But people will never forget how you made them
    feel."

--Maya Angelou

Anchor House

Anchor House was founded in 1978 by a group of concerned citizens, to help move homeless and runaway youth off the streets of Trenton and reunite them with their family.

Today, Anchor House offers a myriad of comprehensive, life-saving programs and services to more than 1,000 youth and their families each year.

Their mission is to provide a safe haven where abused, runaway, homeless, and at-risk youth and their families are empowered to succeed and thrive. The anchor is used as a metaphor, representing a ship dropping its anchor as a safe place to rest and wait out the storm.

For more information or to learn how you can help, please visit their website

www.anchorhousenj.org

Or contact:

482 Centre Street
Trenton, NJ 08611
Tel: 609.396.8329
Email: info@anchorhousenj.org

Anchor
House

Acknowledgments

This book would not be possible without the women who have stepped into my life at all the right times, and who unknowingly raised me to become who I am today.

A special thank you to Mrs. Sedia, for believing in this book long before I did and for your continued support. You and Mr. Sedia are the reason this book even got written. For years, you have encouraged me to write a book, but I kept putting it off, always saying I couldn't do it because I would need help. Thank you for not giving up and for pushing me to write. This would never have been shared, if it weren't for you.

Thank you to Catherine Sewnig, who encouraged me to use my voice and become a speaker, in order to help not only those who have faced trauma but for teachers to see how they make a greater impact in the lives of kids than they think they do.

Thank you to my husband and kids for their support. Thank you to my daughter for being my biggest cheerleader, and for helping me to see that

I was "raised" by these incredible women. For showing me and telling me that she loves the way we raised her and that I am a great mom.

Thank you to my cousin Kim, who has always been and continues to be there for me. Knowing that you believe in me, support me, and always stand up for me means more to me than you could ever know.

To my circle of friends, who are now my chosen family, thank you for always being there to lift me up when I am in doubt. For your continued support and encouragement for writing this book and sharing my story.

Thank you to Micheal Elchoness for helping me see my self-worth and pushing me when I think I'm not good enough in the speaking world.

Thank you to Ann Kagarise from the *Real Talk With Tina and Ann* podcast, whom I know I was meant to meet. Thank you for your friendship. Thank you for continuing to have me guest host with you and for bringing to the audience topics no one talks about. You have helped me to feel less alone by sharing your experiences and your emotions. I thank you from the bottom of my heart.

I want to thank Ernest Bowker for helping with edits on this book. Thank you, Kathryn F. Galán, for helping to pull all of the pieces together so that this book could come to life.

Thank you to Jess Ekstrom for believing and supporting women speakers and authors.

A special thank you to Derek Clark for your words of encouragement and guidance. Along with all of my 30-second moments, it has made a lasting impact.

Last but not least, I want to thank Michelle McLaughlin-Watt for loving me unconditionally since I was fourteen years old. For being my constant. And for helping me to see all of the caring people around me. If it weren't for you, I would not have been able to see and feel the power in a 30-second moment. I can't imagine what my life would be like, if I didn't have you. I love you to the moon and beyond!

About the Author

Denise Bard is a mother and motivational speaker living in the Baltimore-D.C. area. She has long been a special-needs advocate, sitting on panels and committees for military families helping to advocate for those who don't have a voice.

She sits on the board of directors of Anchor House, where she sheltered as a teenager, and speaks about childhood trauma, her challenging times growing up, and the deep impact of just 30-second moments from women in her life who gave her hope, inspiration, and the determination to live through that day. They helped her become the wonderful mother she is to her two young adult children and now to give back to her community, inspiring teachers to find their 30-second moments and support a new generation of young people.

www.ingramcontent.com/pod-product-compliance
Lightning Source LLC
Chambersburg PA
CBHW051105250726

48656CB00001B/487